DUNES REVIEW

EDITORIAL BOARD

Thank you to this issue's Patron, Bronwyn Jones.

COVER IMAGE :
"The Spotted Turtle" by Dani Knoph Davis
Image courtesy of the artist.

DUNES REVIEW

VOLUME 27 ISSUE 2

DECEMBER 2023

CONTENTS

Land Acknowledgement

Dunes Review is published on the traditional lands of the Grand Traverse Band of Ottawa and Chippewa Indians. It is important to understand the long-standing history that has brought us to reside on the land, and to seek to understand our place within that history. We thank the Anishinaabe people for allowing us to be here today.

Cover Artist's Statement

The Spotted Turtle is a rare but mighty site in Michigan. During the past century and a half, the boggy habitats required by these turtles have been drained significantly or developed for human use. In addition to development, pollution, pet trade exploitation, nest predation, and road mortality now denote this species as threatened in the Great Lakes region and legally protected in the State of Michigan.

Learn more about the Spotted Turtle at Michigan Natural Features Inventory: https://mnfi.anr.msu.edu/

Making time to be in nature and learn about wildlife inspires my work. My detailed watercolor illustrations are an expression of reverence for wildlife. Growing up in Michigan, I cherished time on the lake, looking for bass and turtles, observing clams, and searching for Monarchs in the meadows. After attending the School of Art & Design at the University of Michigan, I relocated to Seattle where I illustrated and sold my first collection of salmon paintings. Working with small round brushes and many layers of transparent watercolor washes, I developed a style of illustrating species inspired by the artists of natural history. In 2012, I put down roots in Northern Michigan where I continue to develop a collection of Michigan wildlife illustrations including trout, turtles, butterflies, and birds.

—Dani Knoph Davis

Editors' Notes

We've written about this before: as we go through the submissions, themes begin to emerge. It's a kind of magic that infuses our process of shaping each issue. This time around, I saw a pattern of seeing, of characters or speakers seeing things in a new way. Changing perspective is an essential ingredient in literature to begin with. But in this batch, I was struck by the variety of ways in which speakers re-saw or re-imagined. Our cover art, by the northern Michigan artist Dani Knoph Davis, underscores that idea. "Every species has a story," she says. Take a look at the creatures, the stories, the miracles all around us. We hope you find some new ways of seeing in this issue. Thanks, as always, for your support.

— Teresa Scollon

Don't we just love heartbreak? Not while we're in it, of course, not when we're confined by its stifling grip, unable to see past our own fingertips—but later, years later, with the perspective granted by time, when regret feels like a foreign word and we can revel in the nostalgia of past missteps and losses. Then, it's not so hard to love memory; it's a gift to have walked the path to where we are.

This issue begins with what I read as an homage to those memories. *This is how he spreads out / the limbs of nostalgia*, writes Nathan Lipps, *that sickness he returns to.* The pieces in this issue take me to that place—that indulgent sickness—nudging certain memories closer to my surface, breaking my heart in the way the best poems and stories can. I hope that you too will let yourself be still in the spaces ahead, crack open a little, let the heartbreak be a reminder of what it means to be alive.

—Jennifer Yeatts

Nathan Lipps
VULTURES IN THE SYCAMORE WAITING FOR WHAT WE HOPE TO HALT

In the morning carrying a rake
across his shoulder
hand stretched to the handle
soft with use
until here is the spot
& leaning into it
his breath smoke in early spring
forehead damp & cold
& too hot yet
this is how he spreads out
the limbs of nostalgia
that sickness he returns to
flowers blooming
& winter & already the sun
a super nova even now all things
too late. His friends
have told him
regrets are pointless
Perhaps he thinks
watching a deer edge along
nosing the frosted green
searching uncertain for what
has been distorted
by our love for memory
Perhaps he says quietly
but aloud into the air
reaching out with the rake
its tines braiding a year
his breath the origin
of fire & the deer lifts her chin
& the vulture prepares its nest

Zoe Boyer
THE MORNING AFTER

I know I'm meant to say
it all looked better come morning,
something about a sober mind and
limpid light, dawn blushing the lake.

New day, fresh start — as if
I've awoken someone who
won't hunger for alteration,
who won't do it again.

This life doesn't want clarity,
it wants a bleary-eyed appraisal,
vaseline on the lens, a trick
to make the world's sharp edges
appear soft and forgiving.

Maybe you'd rather hear
about revelation, or the bridal lace
of cresting waves, the elegance
of a heron perched lithe-legged
on the break-wall?

But there are twenty seagulls
fighting over a Dorito in a hash
of feathers, riding high in chase,
loosing pink-throated screams,
unconcerned with dignity, with
the hushed beauty of daybreak.

Have you ever seen anything
so magnificent as this
naked wanting, every grace
given over to the fleeting thrill?

Spent bottles flame like torches
in the sand, burning down toward
a distant evening, the hours fraught
and plodding; I want what quickens,
the winged blur, easy distance.

Rae Zalopany
THE INEXPLICABLE CREATION
OF A TWO-PERSON COVEN

I grab the bowl we mix pancake batter in and make him place the ingredients into it since it's his spell: two eggshells, an amethyst, one of Porkbun's dropped whiskers, and an unmeasured amount of rosemary and lavender. Harry is uncharacteristically timid with this task as if he's going to fuck up the spell and turn us both green. It's nine o'clock at night and thirty minutes past his bedtime, but I couldn't send him to bed when I know how it feels to be seven years old, to be scared and stare at the shapes your dirty laundry pile makes in the corner of your room. What I'm trying to say is—I didn't start the day out thinking my son and I would be doing witchcraft together. At least, not today.

I realize I'll eventually need the bowl back, plus it felt weird to leave it open and gaping beneath his bed, so I dump marinara sauce into a plastic bag and rinse out the jar to transfer the spell ingredients. I hear our neighbors out back smoking cigarettes and wonder if they can see us through the cracks of our translucent back curtains. They definitely heard us the other night when Harry asked me to cleanse him with my lavender bundle. What did they think when I opened the door to let the smoke out while saying to my seven-year-old, "From the tips of your toes to the top of your head, release any negative energy."

We're making a spell jar to banish his nightmares and Jesus Christ I hope this works.

Harry's eyes grow big when I light the black candle. They grow even bigger when I hand it to him, "Your spell, your seal."

Black is for protection.

Black is for banishment.

Black can be for Invocation.

When we moved into our condo, I noticed little things. The door to my son's room had a repaired patch where someone must've kicked it in. His door locked from the outside. It was colder than any other room. Our first night in the condo, I suggested to my then-boyfriend now-husband, Tyler, that I should sleep with Harry in his new room, "To make sure he feels comfortable and safe." Harry and I'd spent the first three years of his life sleeping together in my childhood room, and as much as my two-person family was gaining by adding Tyler into our lives, I still felt a sense of loss. I would miss the pressure Harry's head made when he inevitably snuggled onto my back. How I could whisper at any point during his REM sleep, "I love you" and he would always whisper, "Love you." That first night in his room in the condo, I dreamt of a man standing in the corner of the room. In the morning while Tyler was making breakfast, I asked Harry how he'd slept.

"I had scary dreams."

"What'd you dream about?"

"I dreamt there was a man standing outside the window."

Outside, I reasoned to myself, was at least a little better than inside.

I cannot help but feel a little guilty that we're in this predicament partially because of me. I don't know if we have a ghost or entity or anything like that, but his room has an energy. The part that's my fault, my dad's fault, my great-great grandfather's fault, is having passed on the ability to feel ghosts or sense them or I don't know, maybe we're just lunatics. I don't care if you do or don't believe me, it is what it is. My husband wasn't a believer, still doesn't want to believe, and I don't blame him. He told me his only experience with the supernatural was waking up once and seeing a tiny, little version of his grandmother on the bedside table sitting on a rocking horse.

The candle feels heavy in my hand, a memory or collection of memories seeping into me like an open blood oath. Somehow, I find myself apologizing internally, but I stop myself since I don't want to put my feelings into this spell. I haven't done magick work besides the cleansing in a long time. It feels like there's an audience in my empty family room waiting for me to do something bad. To be open again, to invoke. I've never practiced magick that wasn't baneful before; I've never held a black candle for good.

The thing is, I know the splendor and wonder of what invocation brings. I see the same curiosity in my son that I'd had as a child for anything otherworldly. My parents wouldn't call themselves pagans, but that's what we are: Hawaiian hapas who celebrate the solstice, and acknowledge the moon, and ask the forest to grant us safe passage. As a child I wanted more. I started practicing astral projection at ten, discovered blood magick by thirteen. When you don't have guidance in spell work and ghosts, well, you don't know the ramifications. Your curses rebound, your body left open becomes available for other things, dark energy attracts dark matter.

"Close your eyes and feel your intention," I say to Harry as the wax drips in methodical blips along the rim of the jar. He holds onto it with both hands, eyes shut tight. He looks like he's praying or pre-sneezing.

I think often about how adults forget about the ghosts and the magick from our childhood. How their ghosts later in life become God and holier ghosts. But dream-demons have been around for a long time, longer than biblical ghouls. Gilgamesh was dreaming of the Humbaba long before we were hyper-intellectualizing the content of our psyches. It's my belief that spirits and energy are endemic in our world. We can interfere with them—to bind, repel or compel them. Sure, the sleep demon by the creek that told me my parents were dead could have been my anxieties and realizations of mortality as a six-year-old. But that same monster wouldn't let me wake up, and when I finally did come to, I heard him laugh and felt the phantom limbs grab for me as I ran from my bed to my parents. It felt real, real as any other person in any other country who dreamt up the Kikimora, Baku, Sandman, Melino, Succubus, and so on.

"Can you put it under my bed?" Harry asks, to which I reply no, not because I don't want to but because I'm trying to break the habit of doing things for him.

"It's your charm, you've got to be the one to do it."

He grabs the jar and walks away, flipping every light switch on, his own little Virgils guiding him to his room. My husband, who is in the other room building a gaming computer, checks out the jar Harry shows him as if it were a Raphael painting that Harry had skillfully crafted. Whatever it is—a charm, a talisman, a placebo—I hope it works.

As a kid, I'd run into my mother's room and even though the nightmares never stopped next to her, I felt safe. She'd buy me little tokens—dice, a preserved four-leaf clover, a blown-glass dandelion— as talisman. But night after night I'd still run into her room, and she'd welcome me into the bed with a scoot towards my father and stroke my hair and tell me to think of white light.

When I was pregnant at twenty-one, I was considering adoption. Young, alone, and convinced I couldn't be the mother he needed me to be, I met my son's prospective adoptive parents, Rick and Steve, at a park pavilion and asked them, "Do you believe in ghosts?" They were everything I wasn't: married, academics, homeowners, Protestant. I dreamt a lot during that pregnancy but not when I was asleep. Driving, I'd dreamt of holding my son's foot while he babbled. At the beach, I dreamt of my son singing horribly at a school play. I'd rub my stomach while my son slept like I was his own personal wraith. With each stroke of my hands, I tried to put as much power into my palms, tried to dispense all my love in touches he couldn't feel.

In the end, I wrote Rick and Steve a letter saying, *"I'm sorry, I can't."*

If the spell is just a collection of items, then it's a collection of items that hold the power of a seven-year-old's hopes and wishes and the reason for a noticeable easiness that comes over him when I tell him it's time for bed. Inexplicably, my son became my own sort of charm, a fae light of sorts, formed from my blood and bones and tissue and lots of French toast.

His neon stars shine down from the ceiling as I bend down to kiss him goodnight, but unlike most nights, he doesn't grab onto my arm and beg me to stay.

Linda Nemec Foster
DAWN ON LAKE HURON:
THIS BOY, THIS LIGHT, THIS WATER

Maybe he believes this
arc of light belongs to him.
The glistening water
that dances before
his eyes and waits for his
every measured step. This blue silver
water that silently
embraces him
as if he was a tamer of waves, first-born
son of the first-born ocean.
This boy, this light, this water.
On this day, all three elements are one:
not even the mother can tell them apart.

David Porter
PANGEA

It is nearly midnight.
My wife and son
have dissipated into sleep.
I am moored at the soft give
of her shoulders,
where a tattoo of her first initial
entwines with that of her first love;
beside it a mole the color of topsoil
is a constellation of a single star.
Her tank top has ridden up her ribs.
I touch the skin along her stomach,
and she pushes my hand away without waking.
He is ringlets and a pacifier,
propped against three pillows
In the crook of her left arm.
Soon after dawn
he will thrash until he wakes
and drive us from sleep.

We have slipped into some cool pocket,
a path through the woods,
and we stroll along, whistling, even,
certain no one will see us,
certain not a soul knows where we are.
We are a single continent,
bounded by an unbroken coastline.
I want to live forever
in the forest of their flesh.

Ellen Welcker
GOOGLE SPECIAL PLOVER

My searches get dumber
and yet: Piping Plover.
Never having seen one, I learn
what I see, mating and keening
at the YMCA, are Killdeer. Thanks,
Google. Still special, just not
endangered, and yay. After,
on small stilts stalking
the gravel toward my parking spot
near her nest, I assume, and assume
my Attenborough: "Extraordinary—",
former sad weedy strip transforms
in eye of poet to sacred nesting grounds
of small, ordinary but previously thought
special plover. This is a nature poem.
We were parked to play pickleball.
We like to play, my child and me,
when there's a little, not a lot, of time
—happily not enough time—
to be productive. Better to wander
midtown's creek, peek a crawdad, lie
beneath a tree, fish behind the seat
for something to toss about, think. When you hit
a pickleball, it's called a "dink," so that's perfect
for our purposes—a word with a wink.
We begin to banter and dink and giggle
and quick as a blink it's over, our time.
This is what I thought we'd do
that day we spied the Killdeer,
but what happened instead
was the mating, then a dink,
then sobbing, such sobbing and tears
about killing and dying and having
named these fears, screaming
and hurling his racket. Which skidded
in gravel toward Killdeer's nest.

(no break)
Who cried right back and ruffled her feathers
as idiotically I noted this idiom's fount.
Can you believe this is a nature poem,
but yes, it has everything: parking lot
ecosystems, anthropocentrism,
mimicry, bluff charges, wonder, delight,
blunder and terror and sex and death
and blight, a howling child, a writer
so full of mother: so full of folly,
love, and sorrow she can barely.

Terry Bohnhorst Blackhawk
MY EX AND I SEEK A WEDDING VENUE FOR OUR SON

Devasadhan Mandir, Detroit, Michigan

We were tired. The day was long and it had barely begun.
We walked the grounds of the Fischer family's leftover
mansion — Hare Krishnas ran it now — and heard the peacocks
barking, caterwauling, hollering. Were we the stranger danger
they were warning of? We tried the Krishna Café but found
the tables too small, the menu lacking. Blossoms of the Catalpa
Bean Tree — O Caterpillar Tree, O Cigar Tree — swelled like orchids,
waltzed the air like moths, but what was it embezzled the breeze,
kept us from linking arms, hands, purpose? Dear Lord Vishnu,
had he resolved to be rid of me even then? The lawn swept down
to a canal off the river where sailboats, festooned with flags,
were forming a regatta. In another time, we might have loved
to lollygag there, in another life not hobbled by each other.

Barbra Nightingale
FULL BODY PET SWAN

AutoCorrect changed *scan* to *swan*
and I am gliding on water,
impervious to passersby.

I gaze at the stones
drowned by the lake, contemplating.
Like a Buddha, I sit and wait.

Somehow, I've swallowed the clouds,
their white fluff coursing like sugar
in my veins, racing to parts feathers do not reach.

A person with X-ray vision might see
my quickly beating heart, my hollowing bones,
all my secrets revealed.

The slow ride into the cylindrical tube
like drifting under a bridge, where people
throw pellets purchased for a quarter,

hoping for a flash of wing,
dip of a long, white neck,
squawk of acknowledgement.

A beginning in disguise,
I paddle away, exhale
clouds, filling the sky.

JC Reilly
CUTTHROAT CHESS

for GA

Morrissey's voice hangs desultorily on the air, and you
and I play another round of chess-to-the-death. You shut
down the deliberate advance of my knight, your
queen flying from the other side of the board. I mouth
a curse as she takes him out. I rally my bishop, think as how
our relationship has devolved to afternoon chess fights. You can
not stand it now I've started reading chess books, and you
begin losing game after game. Furious as the impotent king, you say
I'm cheating, accuse me of introducing chaos in the game—as if I
want to play like a master. I don't. I just don't want to go
on losing. Not when you crow about winning, or swan about
the apartment and throw your wins in my face like fish. Things
do not go well for us as I progress—but we keep playing the
game, day after day after day. This afternoon, another wrong
step on my part—castling kingside. The way
your lips straighten, torpedo-thin, in protest! You think I
have invented an illegal move but I know I am
building on my strategy to win. I am no longer human
girl but a machine of remembered rules and clever plays, and
I take piece after piece like I'm mowing down the royal court. I
can't help give in to my new-found power, where I need
to win more than I need to keep you as a friend. To
dangle my skill like a plum becomes the goal, not just before you, but be-
fore all three of your roommates, who had loved
me at the beginning of the year but now think me just
as big a jerk as you. Even when I could earn a win, like
today, you knock your king over—deny me true victory. Everybody
here hates us now, because we resort to shouting. No one else
need know how my heart is breaking, for a game, for you—as it always does.

A Golden Shovel after The Smith's "How Soon is Now"
(*Meat is Murder*, 1985)

Amanda Russell
LAST I SAW YOU

for a poet friend

Between my Diet Pepsi
and your Japanese food,
we leaned closer,
to keep our words
from being swallowed
by guitar solos.

The top of your hair barely
brushed the side of mine.
And when the waiter asked,
you added a request

for kimchee sauce —

Now *there's* a recipe for bridging absence
to meet need, a recipe for holding on
though Earth turns her head away
from the sight
of the sun.

Pickling is one way to keep the unkeepable.

But there was no time left to talk about that.
Nor did we discuss what distance does

because we sat in the em dash of June —
because for this minute we were together
despite what's to come.

A swan song, you called it.
I didn't know what that was.

Joannie Stangeland
STILL

After his body was bagged, taken away,
his parents on a plane approaching,

I sat on the sofa he recently left.
Across the room, the fish tank burbled
a plume of luminous planets.

Fluid had filled his lungs.
His last breath, I did not hear.

Chilled, I turned the heat up high, higher.
Shock made the air shimmer, glisten —
and in that word, listen

to air rising through water.
I would tell you a story less harrowing,

but each December brings me back to this —
the fish, their delicate fins, their busy mouths,
as air and water defined us,

binding him to me more closely
than marriage, than children,

that night giving no safe harbor.

Greg Rappleye

D.H. LAWRENCE AT *ROSA'S TACOS*, ALONG THE RIVER ROAD, OUTSIDE OF TAOS, NEW MEXICO

"If I were the moon, I know where I would fall down."
                                    -D.H. Lawrence, *The Rainbow*

I saw him there just last Tuesday,
thin and pale, stifling a cough
behind his napkin and barbacoa wrap,
otherwise sitting quietly at a yellow picnic table
with squirt bottles of pico de gallo and salsa verde.
The air was redolent of cumin and sizzling pork
and the Freightliners on their way to Albuquerque
and Santa Fe were slowing down,
downshifting through the spicy sweetness
of the warm air and lazy noon-hour traffic.
His brown hair lifted slightly in the wash
of a passing semi, its double-pups
groaning through an achy gear shift
and a tap of air brakes as he bit into the warm
barbacoa and reached for the green sauce,
his tongue just touching his lower lip.
"*Madre de Cristo,*" he whispered,
rising from the yellow table,
"that's *muy bueno*! If I was ravenous (which I am),
and if I were the moon," he said, "(which I am not),"
his arms spreading as if to embrace every aspect
of Rosa's patio, her potted cacti, his diet Coke
and the Fords and pickups in the gravel parking lot
beyond, "I know where I would fall down."

Nancy Squires
NASA SENDS PICTURES TO MY FEED—

Today, a lonely-looking globe
hanging out in space
it's Pluto, where a day
is 153 hours
imagine waiting half of them
for night to fall
Pluto's atmosphere expands
when near the sun, shrinks
when far away—kind of how
I feel about my friends in Florida
who tease me via text
about the weather here
I call to hear their voices
which make my heart expand
Pluto
has an orbit that's way out there
one trip around the sun,
248 Earth-years
without a birthday party—luckily
it's got moons
to keep it company
it spins backwards
does Pluto
science calls this motion retrograde
I call it remembering—I do it
more and more
Oh Pluto
your status seems to ping-pong
like a look
going in and out of fashion
we see you, little sometimes planet
chin up—only 75 hours
'til morning.

Dave Hardin
POEMS

Like Icelandic *Huldufólk* or the morel,
You can search but they refuse to be found
Until it suits their purpose; unknowable
As God's will. Rare as life, unmediated

By screens. I caught a glimpse last week,
Rounding the corner down the liquor aisle,
But it was gone like bourbon and branch
On Derby Day, or the name of the actor

From that series streaming on the service
I keep threatening to cancel. I'll see one
Lurking outside the window now and again
When I'm gazing at everything and nothing,

But they're scarce as a whippoorwill crooning
The Ides of March when I'm staring down
My father in the hourglass of the bathroom
Mirror. Slapping pockets for the Moleskine

Napping in my other jacket feels like fanning
On a three-two pitch when one alights, or fades
In the rearview mirror, shopping cart groaning
With lost gems crammed into Hefty bags.

Garrett Stack
AIRPORT

The taxi driver is strapped
so his 9mm jiggles
in his gym shorts
as he loads up my luggage. He asks
where I'm in from
and I don't tell him
about starting the day watching swells
break over the hopeful boards
of six keiki and their uncle
surfing up with the sun
because all I can think of
in the dark back seat
on that asphalt ocean
is the term *pancake holster*
how innocent it sounds,
tasty even. All this travel has made me
metaphorical, like this airport
which allowed me to cross a continent
only to end up pulled along
on a different kind of tide
facing the other side
of night
or like this day
which began with water
and ends with ammunition.

John Flesher
A STAB OF CONSCIENCE

Wooden stairs creaked as we descended to the dank basement. I was maybe ten years old, and we were visiting my grandparents' home in the little Missouri town where Dad grew up during the Depression, joining the Navy a few months before the end of World War II. He'd promised to show me something he brought home from Japan, and now the ceiling bulb illuminated an object hanging on a nail protruding from the cement wall. He took it down, brushed off a layer of dust and a cobweb or two, gripped the handle and drew the blade from its scabbard of canvas and leather.

"A sword!" I gasped.

"No," he replied, "it's called a bayonet," which was something of a letdown, although I didn't say so. Swords were cool. Robin Hood and Zorro dueled with swords. But I'd never heard of a bayonet. To my boyish ears, the word seemed ill-suited to a deadly weapon—too *pretty*, somehow. Until Dad explained how it's fastened to the muzzle of a rifle and thrust at your enemy in frenzied, hand-to-hand, kill-or-be-killed combat, and suddenly I was staring in awe. I took hold of it, ran my fingers along the cold steel, tapped the dull but still imposing tip. There were no guns in our household, so this probably was the first time I had touched anything made for the express purpose of shedding human blood. Maybe that made an impression. Something about it still does.

Dad had been among millions of servicemen massed to invade the Japanese home islands, only to be reprieved by the war's sudden end. He spent a year with the U.S. occupation forces. But had things turned out differently, this bayonet—or one like it—might have been the end of him. For this was a Japanese bayonet, stockpiled with other weaponry to repel the American assault. It was intended to kill my father-to-be, destroy him amid hellish explosions, shots and screams on a blood-soaked beach or city street. Instead, two atomic bombs fell from the sky. Two hundred thousand people were killed instantly, mortally wounded, or doomed to slow death from radiation sickness. Japan surrendered. The kid who would become my dad found the bayonet while helping clear out a munitions warehouse in Sasebo, thirty miles from the toxic ruins of Nagasaki. He took it home and hung it on the basement wall.

After his parents died and their house was sold, he gave the bayonet to me. I stored it in my own cobwebby basement in northern Michigan, on a shelf alongside cardboard boxes of yellowed newspaper clippings, old love letters, random memorabilia. Now and then I'd wrench the bayonet from its sheath, look it over, finger the blade.

My wife and I have a makeshift wine cellar down there. One afternoon I descended to fetch a bottle: a local pinot noir, elegant and dry. A nice pairing with our dinner of grilled salmon and asparagus, fresh from the farmers' market. My eyes fell on the bayonet, there on the shelf. I recently had visited Dad and thumbed through his scrapbooks from Japan, and now my mind wandered to the bombs, the obliterated cities, the two hundred thousand people killed—and me, alive and well in a musty basement halfway around the world.

The nuclear horror was unleashed, and the war abruptly ended. My father-to-be came home. I would be born. Grow to manhood. Marry and become a dad myself. Grill salmon and sip wine on pleasant summer evenings in the shade of a towering backyard oak.

Survivor's guilt? I don't think so. I am lucky indeed, like many other white middle-class American men, but feel no need to offer empty apologies over arbitrary twists of fate.

Yet something gnawed at me to take that bayonet upstairs, from darkness to light, and place it on a bookshelf in my home office, where it often catches my eye. I sense that it's returning my gaze, this instrument of death that has never seen battle, now reduced to an object of curiosity, a conversation piece, but still capable of fulfilling its original mission. I sense it would tell me something if it could, and wish I knew what it was. Or think I do. But there is only silence.

❀ ❀ ❀ ❀

The name is believed to have derived from the French city of Bayonne, where the bayonet dates to the sixteenth century. According to researcher Ralph E. Cobb, it was created to hunt wild boar—which, unlike most game animals, tends to charge its would-be killer. So unwieldy were flintlock muskets of those days that, if you merely wounded the swine with your first shot, it might slash you with razor-sharp tusks before you could reload. The *baionnette a manche* greatly improved the hunter's odds. Jam it into the tip of your rifle and, presto, you've got a spear. It didn't take military strategists long to figure out that such a tool would come in handy on battlefields.

Early "plug bayonets" were inserted directly into the gun barrel, but you could no longer fire. Then came the "socket" bayonet, affixed to the muzzle without blocking the bullet, enabling the soldier to shoot and stab at will. Its first documented use in Europe was during the Thirty Years' War. A century later, his beleaguered army advancing on Trenton, New Jersey, for a must-win attack on the British, George Washington received a message from General John Sullivan that his troops' gunpowder was damp from snow and sleet. "Tell General Sullivan to use the bayonet," Washington replied. "I am resolved to take Trenton." He did, sparing the fledgling American revolution from death in the cradle.

These days, rifles and artillery pack such firepower that troops are more likely to use a bayonet to open a beer bottle than kill the enemy. Yet it was used as recently as 2009, when a lieutenant with the Royal Regiment of Scotland exhausted his ammunition and charged a Taliban fighter in Afghanistan, running him through. The Scotsman was awarded the Military Cross for "exemplary gallantry."

❖ ❖ ❖ ❖

I, meanwhile, have never been in a fight, aside from a few playground skirmishes as a kid and a tussle in college with a guy who tried to snatch my girlfriend's purse. Remarkable, isn't it? All those people killed or wounded in violent conflicts since Cain slew Abel and I've never had to fight, really fight, for life or country or anything else. This has resulted largely from fortuitous timing. Consider the January morning in 1973 when my ninth-grade world history teacher, a thirty-something dude with Elvis sideburns who wore bell-bottom slacks as we kids did, strolled into the classroom and asked if we'd seen President Nixon's speech the night before, announcing the end of the Vietnam War. "You've been spared," he added cryptically.

Enough of us exchanged bemused glances that he felt obligated to explain: "Now you don't have to worry about going to Vietnam yourselves someday."

That might have been the first time it dawned on me that I could have been among those guys riddled with machine gun bullets or blown apart by land mines or tortured to insanity in a POW camp in a sweltering jungle infested with pythons and rats, where they fed you only a watery bowl of pumpkin soup or a few spoons of rice a day. I might even have been disemboweled with a bayonet. I seem to recall a quivery, chilling sensation while contemplating such fates, but it passed quickly, and I resumed thinking about baseball and girls.

I now wonder: If the war had still been raging four years later, when I turned eighteen, would I have enlisted? I grew up in a conservative North Carolina community with tobacco farms, Jesse Helms commentaries on local TV, and Klan billboards on the outskirts of town (they finally came down in the Seventies). And, significantly, an Air Force base. My nascent political outlook was right-wing; I might have considered it my Christian American duty to take on the godless communists. But I was college-bound and presumably could have gotten deferments, as Dick "I had other priorities" Cheney and other hawkish types managed. Funny how attractive war can seem when somebody else does the fighting. I'd probably have been spared. Again.

✿ ✿ ✿ ✿

Instead, I became a journalist. Woodward and Bernstein were inspiring a new generation of reporters to gird for combat with the powerful and corrupt. I just wanted to write stories—and got my wish.

But journalism can be dangerous work. According to the Committee to Protect Journalists, 2,286 had been killed worldwide between 1992 and early this year. The wounded—mentally and physically—are countless. I was posted in Washington when fellow Associated Press reporter Terry Anderson was freed after nearly seven years as a hostage in Lebanon. Among his first stops was the D.C. Associated Press bureau. I was struck by the sheer ordinariness of the man, less than a week removed from captivity in a foul cellar, kept hungry and haunted by the ever-present specter of death. His handshake was gentle, his voice mild. Shorter than average, like me. Smiling yet a bit reserved, perhaps still dazed, Lazarus blinking in the sunlight after emerging from the tomb. As he turned to greet another colleague, I patted his shoulder and felt his muscles tighten.

By those standards, my long, eventful career has been rather tame. No war zones, no death threats (that I know of, although I avoid Twitter and similar internet cesspools). I've been cursed, kicked off people's property, doused with pepper spray during a protest. I've taken measured risks: flying in rickety aircraft to observe wolf packs, getting too close for comfort to floods and forest fires. Back in 1994, I squeezed into a sixteen-foot submersible craft and descended to the bottom of Lake Superior to gaze at the Edmund Fitzgerald's mangled carcass. Dark, desolate, haunting, a grave for twenty-nine mariners. Only recently, after the Titan imploded near the Titanic wreckage in the North Atlantic, did I ponder how dangerous our mission had been. The Fitzgerald was five hundred and thirty feet down, much shallower than the Titanic. Yet if our sub had snagged or stalled, no one could have rescued us before the oxygen ran out. At the time, my biggest concern was that a competing reporter had talked her way onto one of the dives and if I couldn't match her story, I might as well be dead anyway. I jawboned the crew leader into making room for me.

Were such episodes "fights?" I never really thought of my work as such, even when scrapping for information with government bureaucrats and corporate PR flacks, challenging evasive politicians or digging through mountains of inscrutable documents for evidence of malfeasance. Rather, I considered myself a chronicler of other people's battles: the candidates, clashing in elections; the families of children lost to war, disasters or crime, grasping for sanity; the racial minorities and LGBTQ people, crusading for justice; the environmentalists, struggling to preserve the only place humans can live.

And more: the oil drillers, miners, and loggers, fearful that their jobs and way of life would disappear; the white, straight, middle-aged hairdresser in yoga pants with a stars-and-stripes Trump logo who likened trans people to pet-shop animals in a social media post and insisted to me that she was the real victim after protesters picketed her strip-mall salon. Shortly after the 1995 Oklahoma City bombing, I listened for two hours in stunned silence as a leader of the Michigan Militia pleaded with me to report the "real facts": it had been the work of the Japanese government, in retaliation for a sarin gas attack on the Tokyo subway system—masterminded by the CIA! It was obvious! Why was the media hiding the true story from the world?

Good God, I thought. And this man has guns. Lots of guns. But I felt neither anger nor contempt, for him or most other people I've written about, no matter how deranged or odious, and I tried to treat them all fairly. It helped that I was pretty good at the studied neutrality required of mainstream journalists, the kind of emotional detachment that presumably is also important for the likes of judges and surgeons. My job was to not pass judgment or win debates, but to get the story. Just get it. Get it right and write it well and let others react as they wished, then deal with my own feelings later. I took this approach as best I could for forty-three years, and it seemed to work.

Yet now—recently retired, taking stock of what I've accomplished and wondering what difference it made—I feel a nagging sense that somehow it wasn't enough.

You can aim for even-handedness in a society where the concept of objective truth is widely accepted, despite disagreement on the particulars. Where democracy and the rule of law, however flawed, are secure. Where most arguments are settled peaceably. I have practiced my craft under the protection of such a system. What if it collapses, a scenario that doesn't seem so unthinkable these days? Might the fate I've dodged throughout life catch up with me in the end?

I could keep my mouth shut and my head down, travel and play and grill more fish and drink more wine and pretend it's not happening or it's not so bad. Everybody keeps saying we boomers should step aside and let the younger folks run things, right?

My eyes wander again to the bayonet, there on the bookshelf, never used. Suddenly it's as if I can hear it for the first time, stabbing at my conscience.

"You cannot sit this out. No one gets a pass when everything is at stake."

Impulsively I grab it once again, yank it from its sheath, stiff with age. Grip it by the handle. What does it feel like to actually use this thing, to gut someone with it? What kind of savage rage or primal fear would I have to summon? And how must it feel to be on the receiving end—of a bayonet, a bullet, a bomb?

I think of Anselmo, the aging guerrilla fighter in Hemingway's *For Whom the Bell Tolls*, who hates killing the Spanish Republic's fascist enemies and would prefer putting them to work so they can see the error of their ways. The fighter is a peaceful laborer, forced by circumstances to take up arms. He joins a mission to blow up a strategically important bridge, dies heroically, and the good guys lose the battle anyway—and eventually the civil war. Somehow, I can't envision myself holed up in a mountain cave with a resistance cell, making sabotage forays against a totalitarian regime. Still, you never know what you can do until you must. Just ask the Ukrainians.

But I recall another exchange in that novel, where the American protagonist Robert Jordan tells the Spanish guerrillas that his country also has fascists, or people "who do not know they are fascists but will find it out when the time comes." Can't you go ahead and settle their hash now, a Spaniard asks? "No," Jordan replies. "We cannot destroy them. But we can educate the people so that they will fear fascism and recognize it when it appears and combat it."

A nice thought. Perhaps once upon a time it was even true. Edward R. Murrow could command a respectful nationwide audience seventy years ago for his takedown of Senator McCarthy. But now it comes across as sadly naive. Former President Donald Trump has a vast right-wing media arsenal at his disposal, plus an army of keyboard warriors led by the man himself, bombarding us with distortions and lies. How can we teach people to recognize and battle this metastasizing cancer, when so many hang on his every word, do "their own research" and scoff at experts? If they deny the scientists' warnings about climate and Covid, how likely are they to believe the journalists, the poets, the philosophers sounding the alarm about democracy in peril?

What would the bayonet say?

"There's no chance at all, if no one tries."

* * * *

If that little souvenir's mission is to prod me into action, what is mine? To abandon the comfort zone of public neutrality and plunge into the fray with others of good will, using words and reason in desperate hope of preventing bloodshed? What difference will one more voice make amid the crazed din of social media?

I search the web, see names of authors, poets, journalists, imprisoned for challenging authoritarians. Some tortured or killed: Ashraf Fayadh, convicted of apostasy in Saudi Arabia, his sentence of death by beheading commuted at the eleventh hour but still serving eight harsh years with 800 lashes. Galal El-Behairy, driven to hunger strikes and a suicide attempt in an Egyptian prison. On and on. Commonplace in many countries, but not in the United States—for now, although ugly clouds are gathering. Doxxing. Harassment. Threats. They know where you live.

I click away from the latest news story about the former president and his cultish followers, armed and bristling for revenge. They smell blood in the water. I smell dinner cooking. Maybe I really don't need to get involved in this mess. Everything I could say has been said, anyway. I power down the computer, step toward the kitchen. And there's the bayonet again, right in front of me.

"It's not too late. For once in your life, fight for something."

I'm retired, I tell it. Out to pasture.

"Maybe you should just take me back to the basement."

No. Come to think of it, I need you here. Stick around.

FM Stringer
OLD MAGIC

Who's to say it wasn't
Because of the badger skull

You threaded with one
Feather from the horned owl

And buried in the yard
That we were spared

Insofar as we have been spared

Late at night I wake to find you
In the other room

In the dim of the TV muted
In the other life you imagine
You deserve, loveless and ruined

You can't sleep until you touch it
You tell me, the other life
Step inside of it
Are anguished by it
Are anguished by it enough
And come back, settled up

Timber rattler skin (freshly molted)
Cicada husks

Morning—your handwriting
Tense on the list stuck
With a Mickey magnet to the fridge

What is left behind
When the animal moves
From one tiny epoch to its next

Dewclaw casing
White-tail velvet

Outside it's overcast
The leaves in the old oak too
Are beginning their turn

Paper shell of a blue crab
Wool from the American blackbelly

Abhishek Mehta
MY FATHER, THE SWEATER

The kind of depression my father has
is not a modern one, one which speaks
in a known language or can write its own name
and the directions back to the house.
His depression is an old neighbour
that is simple in the head,
has a sweater with a message sewed in at the back.
Please return him to this address.
They always do, always return him.
It holds him so completely, his head is bowed
and eyes look into an assured middle distance,
the kind at the end of which trains arrive
or a backyard rose garden languishes.
It might be the meds too but in our family
we don't ask what is holding what up.
We watch him like a magic trick that's been going on
for twenty years; every time we feel it would end,
there's another "pick a card, remember your card."
We picked all the cards a while ago,
now we pick the anticipation of them.
Some days I wish this sickness really was
a person we could see,
one with the sweater.
We'd dress him up every day in December
in that sweater until one day we won't
and he won't come back.
And we'd lose what we put in him,
what through him we put in another person
that never was.
And then there'd be just him left,
my father, the sweater,
something to remember someone else by.

Alison Swan
MINISTER

Thirteen years have passed since
he has visited seven glaciers,
seven fields of snow that for millennia
accreted each winter
and melted just a little each summer.
He's listened all night to their chorus sung
eastward, where cranes descend
upon prairie afterimages.
They eat leftover corn.
They remember bison.
This night one glacier will sing quietly.
He will cup a hand to his ear and stay awake.
Next day he will sit from dawn till dusk
with his hand on her, pebbly and gritty,
the way snowfall once became
in a prairie city after a long storm
and an interplay of slight warmings
and deep coolings and dust.
He will collect meltwater in his cup.
He will drink it.

for Kim Stanley Robinson

Bryn Gribben
NASTURTIUM

Feed me less—let me flail
from the hillsides, a fall guy,
summer girl of frilly frock
and full-frame sun hat. Let me
spring up, explode into sunset
on a dollhouse's house—I love
small spaces, don't need my own room
to sprawl. I fling my feelers out
like favors, fashion flayed on
floors after a fete.

Bite my blossom: I'm pepper
to your palate, secret salad
posing as a posy. Give me your
full sun, your worst soil. I'll
cover it—my conquest a tangle
over concrete, crevice, corners.
If the soil here is poor, the only
thing to do is produce and populate,
but I will power the pretty. Pop me
in your mouth and call me savior.

Elizabeth Kerlikowske
TEACHING THE PREPOSITIONAL PHRASE

Where crows glide over August gardens
as cucumber vines cling to deer fences
after morning glories have been eaten by the deer
during fires, under smoke from Saskatchewan
beside the mystery plant we can't identify
until it blooms   Up spruce trees, cones
squirrels will strafe our house with next month
away from the burr-bearing corner
above oat grass, below red buds
out the door cats never use
On moss, inside the embrace of vegetation
under faraway freeway hum
off the fence, acute angle of sunlight
above the pergola, Rose of Sharon
between me and sky, moonflower breath
white trumpets, between shrinking slats
this humdrum paradise.

Eric P. Mueller
JAMES WRIGHT COULD NEVER

Three football players at the front end of the long table in the undergraduate poetry class. One of them stopped playing that season, but that didn't stop the rest of the room, including myself, from seeing him as a football player. One of them was me, still playing even though this was the semester of my horrific knee injury, and the third was my best friend on the team, a fellow offensive lineman. I loved having class with other football players because it meant that I would never feel completely alone—like a lonely bull in a China shop. I had felt like a moose in a small garden while studying humanities, but I would have felt similarly studying economics or something STEM-related, so at least here in the poetry class I was sitting in my preferred bed of flowers.

The poetry professor handed us a new packet of example poems almost every week. He'd split the packets in two piles and pass one to his left and one to his right. Even though all the sheets were identical, it still felt like we received the first pick because we sat close to the professor. It should be a requirement for creative writing classes to take place at a long, brown table; there's something homey about it. One packet was prefaced with the acknowledgement (or warning) that it contained the greatest football poem ever written. I don't remember anyone specifically looking at me or the three of us, but it felt like he was challenging us—me, in particular—to write a better one.

We read James Wright's "Autumn Begins in Martins Ferry, Ohio" aloud in class, and I spent the next few years trying to rise to the poetry professor's challenge. The poem included many elements that the world of football touches on today: community, class dynamics, race, fathers, sons, and the notion of suicide. Every word is integral to the poem. There's no way Wright could have known back then how bad football was for the body, but even in the early 1960s, he knew something was up. All you need to make the greatest poem about football is to define the game in a way that is visual and clear.

The poetry class challenged me to write about subjects other than football. But I thought football was the only thing that made me unique. Only a small portion of the U.S. population has ever played tackle football in the full drag—helmet, shoulder pads, tight capri pants, spiked shoes. An even smaller percentage of that sample has lettered in three years of NCAA football. Football was the only space that felt supportive and embracing of a body like mine—one that was larger than most, soft, and shaped differently. Without football, I was just fat.

Later that term, the poetry professor assigned us each a poet to study closely and write about. He explained that since he was a Doctor of Philosophy, these poets were our prescriptions. He assigned me James Wright. My best friend received Robert Lowell. I was happy to have "the football guy" over the "confessional poet". Later, I wondered if the professor gave me Wright because Wright was low-hanging fruit.

My stanzas were filled with lines about grief and being in the closet. My dad had been diagnosed with cancer when I was a freshman in high school. He had several major surgeries over the course of seven years. One of those surgeries took place seven days before I left for freshman year of college and the football practices that preceded it. His voice box was removed. He went on disability and used a device to speak. Without football, our only time spent together was getting haircuts and (mostly thanks to pleas from my mother) fishing daytrips for Father's Day. With football, we spent hours in the car together going to and from practice. His excitement, which went as far as creating a weekly email blast to all of his contacts about my games, was the first time I felt his pride, and it made me want to be better at football and even play the sport in college.

"Autumn Begins in Martins Ferry, Ohio" is only three stanzas long and appears in Wright's 1963 *This Branch Will Not Break*. Sixty years old, the poem still feels more "now" than "then." The press that published it, Wesleyan, wasn't far from my hometown in southern Connecticut, but the Northwestern Pennsylvania college I went to was much closer to Martins Ferry. I thought I was doing the right thing, playing a physical, gritty sport in a physical, gritty area. I was far from the city of brotherly love, but instead near Pittsburgh, which forged itself in steel and prided itself on its many football championships. The regional dialect was more south than north. In addition to fields with nothing in them, there was camo, chewing tobacco, and French fries in salads. I couldn't help but wonder: if I had ever fit in with the Connecticut crowd who wore preppy sweaters, would I have ventured off so far from home?

It didn't take long for me to learn that Wright's son, Franz was also a prolific poet. They were the first father/son duo to win a Pulitzer Prize. My dad and I did not connect over his two favorite hobbies: fishing and golf. Getting haircuts with Dad was just a little time in the car where we'd listen to sports on AM radio. I didn't speak much to my dad nor the barber who'd we'd seen since I was three years old. I was a quiet boy, and it wasn't until my early twenties that I realized I could actually be a bit of a talker and people wanted to hear what I had to say. Talking on the phone was hard for Dad with his voicelessness, but we chatted through AOL's instant messenger for hours, especially late at night before his sleeping meds kicked in. We didn't have the outside world to deter us from each other. With only words, we were father and son. Of the four of us (James, Franz, Dad, me) I wonder who in addition to me dreamt of heroes and what those heroes looked like. Although my dad was truly heroic, especially after his cancer diagnosis, I never looked at my dad as a hero but more like an ocean — uncontrollable, deep with mystery, brutally harsh at times, and also a source of comfort and healing. I can't ask the Wrights what or who they dream of, but I can read their work.

I took "Forms of Poetry" with the poetry professor after that first workshop. There were no other football players in that class. Each week we studied a new form and wrote a poem in that form's tradition. There was no workshop element to the course, but little groups formed and people traded poems with each other and the professor. I was not a part of any group, but I found writing in the same forms of poetry that folks had written in for hundreds or thousands of years to be a stronger communal feeling than what I was getting from college, home, or any community I came from.

James Wright served up my two favorite turns of phrase in that football poem. Adverbs get a bad reputation, but "gallop terribly" is such a mic-drop of a descriptor. "Gallop" because players are rarely ever treated or seen as people: we are workhorses saddled, reined, and led into war. "Terribly" because all we do or did on the field is hurt ourselves and others, even though it's a game and we're taught that games are meant to be fun. There is truly no ethical way to conduct full-padded, full-contact football.

Of the faculty I could study under for my undergraduate thesis, I went with the poetry professor because he looked at academic study as rigor and, to me, rigor was what made things worth doing. It was how I knew that work was being done. It was especially hard to not write about my knee injury: torn ACL, MCL, meniscus, bone bruising, and a delicate-looking PCL, which happened during a football game on national television. Instead, I wrote about racoons, poison dart frogs, departed young people I read about in the news, and my dying father. Aside from "gallop terribly," the phrase I love most from Wright's football poem is "suicidally beautiful." I was a lover of punk and goth things when off the football field who often wore band t-shirts with black track pants, so of course I loved this line. There is no way to safely collide with someone, no matter how expensive the helmets become. Playing football, especially if you're a lineman like me, like my dad, is the equivalent of bashing a hammer on your head over and over like a *Merry Melodies* cartoon. It's not as funny without the sound effects. I'm not sure what Wright meant by beautiful—whether he was referring to our youth or to the fact that we were a melting pot of people playing a game together. I never felt beautiful, so to be seen that way, especially by men, felt like the first time I wore a precious stone.

In the advanced poetry workshop, I talked a lot about form and content. I followed technique in football and in poetry because I didn't feel like I had God-given talent in either. Coaches referred to me as a technician, someone who does everything "correctly" to make up for other shortcomings. This made me think of my body differently. I thought I had to change the form of my body in order find the acceptance it needed. The form of it—plus-sized, worn-out ligaments, red-headed, bad eyes—how did it relate to the content of me as a person? I wanted to be perfect in my writing technique so that people would want to read my work. This led to a lot of typos, overthinking, and overdone 7,000-word drafts.

A football game, like art, is a moment in time. Each play in a football game is the line of a poem. With twenty-two chess pieces on the field, countless variables make every play unique. Replicating a play in-game is nearly impossible, just as it's nearly impossible to recreate a moment that was truly inspired. The game gets a lot of flak for its stop-and-go cadence, but there's so much to analyze each play that I can watch each one at least five times. The same can be said about lines of poetry, especially the ones we can't stop reading to ourselves over and over. The best coaches are editors of people, assessors of human bodies.

Dad died right before my senior year. I had a creative thesis to write—a book of poems and an analysis of their merit. There were many elegies and poems about being in the closet. I was proud of this poetic endeavor, but I also took my first creative nonfiction course and finally felt like I found home. Poems, like short stories, have so much space for freedom that it can get overwhelming. Nonfiction had parameters I could follow, and it seemed like a great path into storytelling. People write essays about things that they couldn't let go of. In football, holding is a penalty, but players are also encouraged to hold on as best they can without getting caught. It wasn't until years after learning who James Wright was that I even looked into his son Franz and his life. Turns out his dad left him at a young age. Having a rockstar poet parent must have downsides. They experienced many hardships despite their notoriety. I share a few things with my father: irritability, oversensitivity, conflict avoidance, a need to make people laugh, an obnoxiously loud sneeze, a scarred, wrinkled forehead, and an upper lip that grows the same mustache my dad wore for decades. I can't speak much to James and Franz's shared traits aside from writing, but both dealt with substance abuse and maintaining relationships. There's often such a darkness to art that's deemed successful to society, I wondered if good art can come from a place of love and longing.

Franz Wright has a short poem called "To Myself." It's not about football, but it encapsulates my undergrad experience well. I spent so much time driving on route 80, feeling alone, especially after traveling for games hours away from campus, drinking my weight in amber on Saturday nights. "It won't always be like this," Franz said. With Franz Wright, there's a desire to break the cycle and not overtake or become the father. Together, sons can break the cycle that goes back to the ancient Greeks and probably even farther. To do so, we must fearlessly confront what destroys our insides. Franz Wright suggests, "when you begin/ to cough, I won't cover my face,/ and if you vomit this time I will hold you: everything's going to be fine."

In an interview with Kaveh Akbar, Franz mentioned that his dad played semipro football after serving in the Army. It's always cool to hear of a prominent male author from the twentieth century doing anything outside of academia or war, but a football connection is extra special to me. I'm no longer trying to one-up James Wright; he can have the best football poem ever. I cannot follow in his footsteps nor in my own father's. And, despite our common traits, James Wright could never, would never, do what I do, sharing my queer longings and misadventures with arms out open for a hug. I can't talk to James, Franz, or my dad about this, but I consider my writing to be a conversation with them in some way. I'm on a weird little path. I'd like to think that James, Franz, my dad, or even the poetry professor would like my work, me, and who I am becoming.

Bryn Gribben
SELF PORTRAIT AS MY MOTHER'S PERFUME

I am a saxophone of scent, discretion of secretions,
cocktail of bedside clocks,
flocked wallpaper, white paint.

When I push past your hoopla, my absence
snaps your scab like an elastic band—the fabric
of memory is a muscle and an ampersand.

Let me hula hoop your windpipe, washboard your worry,
tuck my galaxy into your neck's balcony
and the chambers of your wrists.

Open a lingerie drawer:
the underbelly of all nightingales flies over and out
across the alley, jungled with grass cuttings and ash.

An olfactory ocelot, I bring you back your lollipop, your bluebottle fly,
your fickle youth unscarred, hiding behind
folding doors that collapse and open like a lung.

I'm the golem, I'm the haint, I'm the letter under the bed,
the leftover Jolly Rancher of your thirteenth Halloween.
I'm in your loveseat, your fibrous and newfound persona.

I was the acorn of your coffin—like knives,
I succumb to what buries itself inside, like books.
I bear the centipede's witness to lopsided illumination,

visions of lichen, of saddle shoes' firm press, a woman walking backwards.

Come with me: witness your moonscape, veer into your made-up
madness, a pinch pot of Boraxo, a pickle barrel of gin gimlets.
I polka-dot your pomegranate with a red even assassins want to wear.

Cradle my crispness like a crow with her jewel—
you can keep us close forever. Luscious lobster
of what's living, I am the resident of the morgue.

Abigail Cloud
LUMBERTOWN

Driving north, I smell for it first,
bracing, dank, what could be rancid butter
or boiled cabbage but isn't; it reeks from the factory
pressing out white, crisp sheets of paper.
My nostrils flaring I picture the churn
of mealy pulp, the smoothing, drying, and wrapping.
I was a child in this city, at holidays visiting
Santa in the mall and bathing in the avocado
green bathtub in my grandmother's house.
It is the irrelevant I wish to remember
most, the possibilities of sea in her bathroom,
the hours spent submarining beneath the green,
the unlikely depth that scared me.
I will feel this fear standing later by her body,

arriving too early and staring down
at the wisps of white hair, soft velour
of her jacket, too-tight press of her mouth.
I will listen vaguely to the home director
while she rambles about the long line of teachers
in my family and how you can see it in our jaw,
my grandmother's, my mother's, my own;
I will wish my mother were there
and escape to find her, and strangely I will know
where to go, a map from childhood
at work in the wheels of my car. I understand
Muskegon, know where Russ's Tele-Dine stands,
how to work the twisted turn into Seaway Boulevard,
or get from the hotel to the funeral home
on a back-road route. Strange to lead my father
down streets he knew long before my birth.
These are like old lumber roads: straight,

white-pine-edged paths where a choice was sliced
into the woods, packed down, turned into railroads
and avenues still carrying the logic of destination.
Later, I will feel drawn back to her old house,
appreciating that it is exactly the same
while others crumble, though the tracks seem closer
to the front steps now. I will have the urge
to climb these steps and call through the ancient
screen door to my grandmother on the horsehair sofa —
in my garage, four years now. It belongs
in this house. Here I learned how cooking gas permeates,
how White Shoulders softens the neck, how rail dust sifts
through the screens with the noise. The train

I have always understood. Each night the cousins climbed
over sleeping parents to peek out of the windows
at its clamorous speed. We watched for the Chessie cars,
waving to their passing cat silhouettes, and wondered
if they knew where they went, and who led them.
I will want them to run past the front porch and rattle me
and my teeth like windows. I know my path,
and later, I will drive homeward, smelling
of funeral, other people's perfumes leached
into my sweater. In one week I will have their illnesses,
my nose blocked, the smell of lumber wedged in deep.

Ellen Stone
GRIEF WANTS EVERYTHING

She came to visit early — before the churr of morning
rustled through her outside clothes, hands clenched

full of sage, rosemary in a paper bag. Soft
balloons were lying round the living room

as if some happiness had ended there. I wanted
to explain we were waiting for what happened

next. That we did not believe in everlasting
like Father and those who came before him.

I wondered why she arrived just then
with herbs and scent, their multitude of uses —

plentitude, profusion, purity. The day felt
so domestic, but we barely offered tea. She sat

quietly as if her breath might lift the pallor
in the air. I thought grief was something moving

through — a visitor who must get somewhere.
I did not know that grief moves in, a roommate

who stays and stays, not asking you for much
at first. Until you see grief wants everything.

We did not think to tell her this, the caller.
She came and sat with us like she already knew.

Joannie Stangeland
TO VISIT MY MOTHER

Gone is the picture window
letting in the western light
and the drapes drawn to prevent the sun
from fading the furniture.
Gone the back room with the piano
and the ironing board, scales
and the smell of steam, the boxes
brought from her mother's farmhouse,
boxes packed with lace and crochet.

Gone, the fire-engine red heads
of geraniums in their pots not wanting
to be moved to the garage, stored
for a winter that felt far away.
Her garage like walking
into the whale's mouth, a place
as cool and dark as memory,
a crate of apricots on top of the freezer — filled
with meats, peaches, berries interred
in plastic — her silvery wrench sets,
her snow tires, push mower,
edger, the water-borer
she stabbed into grass each spring.
My mother without a manicure
kept a well-manicured lawn,
regimented, and penciled debits and credits
disciplined in their columns, my mother
keeping the books like a general,
keeping calico remnants, scraps
for stitching into something,
keeping the spools and bobbins,
the cards of rickrack and edging.

To visit with Mother, in August
or October, was to sweeten your teeth
with apple cake, apple sauce,

(no break)
and the tiny lanterns of raspberries
lighting the backyard where planters
of fuchsias dangled from limbs of the ghost tree
stretching its shadows, tree named
for the seeds that, in fall,
are rattled by wind.

Ellen Stone
HOW I WANT THE ROAD TO YOU

Beached with late February snow
mapping the way home, hill-shorn

back where the barns were full,
all the cows were giving milk

and you not gone underground —
your bed of flour dusted sills,

all the sugar sunk in petals
out the open window. Mother,

here your face is dune-swept
smooth and still, opening

like the sky comes clear
on March days, sudden sun

bearing down — ardent
as if winter never happened.

Perhaps you have gone north
to your Atlantic Ocean

and rest there on its shore,
tidal as the pull toward moon.

Meanwhile the corrugated road
rises up to meet me, rusted

sheds tawny in the afternoon,
wild turkeys hooding the field

and the ditch roaring its way
along the asphalt melting

all that has thawed, loosened
and let go under the ice.

48

Jack Ridl
ALL I KNOW IS IT WAS DARK

And we were walking in the snow, in the four
feet of snow that each winter piles up
along the east side of the house, the flakes

having been blown off the lake, off the roofs,
and into drifts higher than any stocking cap
you had knitted and I had on. Remember? Maybe?

We held hands, well actually gloves,
well, I wore gloves. You had on mittens,
ones you also had knitted. When you knit,

you sit at the end of my grandmother's daybed,
the one as a child I pretended was a bus I drove
every day from the suburbs into the heart of downtown

Pittsburgh after the gray smoke had metamorphosed white.
I didn't know what "The Renaissance City" meant. I knew
only that each day Mrs. Schnelker pulled the cord to be left

off at Seventh Avenue. You are knitting and I am lying
on the daybed, feet on your lap. I keep things clean
where you comb a dry fleece, then pull the wool, set up

your wheel, and spin. That night when we trudged through
the snowfall, glove around mitten, then mitten around glove,
one of us lost our balance. But the other held on.

Eric Torgersen
BABA JUGA

In the dream, *baba juga* meant *big snake*.
My sister who has Alzheimer's
pointed and said it, *baba juga*, and there it was.

In the dream she could still speak.

Once, when we thought
she was just about finished with words,
we told her anyway on FaceTime that we missed her
and she said very clearly in the old voice *I miss myself*.

In the dream she was holding the hand
of a small, somehow *shining* girl,
leading her, I thought, down a steep, descending path,
teaching her words for a new place
and what to watch out for.

But of course it was that girl
leading my sister, who'd lost her way
but could still repeat the lesson, *baba juga*.

I have no idea where that path is;
under my feet already, snakes and all, for all I know.
But how, if I have to, will I find that shining girl
and take her hand?

Michael Mark
EATING A MANGO IN THE HOUSE OF LATKES

She keeps saying *orange-orange*
    and he keeps saying *mango-mango*. Maybe she means
the sunny color – but she keeps laughing,

saying it, so he does too – cutting,
    shearing, welling up as the flappy slices
slide in and out of her mostly toothless mouth, perfumed juice

painting her chin, neck of her only housecoat. Whoever
    heard of such a thing? Feeding an exotic fruit - part cantaloupe,
part sherbet – to his 90-year-old mother

at one in the morning? *Orange-orange. Mango-mango.*
    It's dripping onto the counter, puddling on the linoleum
wetting her bird claw feet.

He read all the doctors' pamphlets. Nothing
    so far will bring back her ability to mend
a torn dress like the-day-before-new, remember

her ghost-language recipes, him. Maybe
    there's a miracle in mangos. She grabs the fish-slippery
flesh from the wood block. She's stopped eating

even her favorites: cottage cheese, boiled chicken, challah.
    At $4 a pound, the mango was a risk. *"Cheap is smart,"*
she taught him. *"Shows respect*

for those who go without and for God, who counts." He cuts
    thinner slivers trying to stretch
her happiness (or distract her from one of her momentary

awarenesses, or himself). She purrs, *orange-orange, orange-orange,*
    takes a piece of rind from the garbage. *Ma!* he shouts,
slips two fingers into her trout mouth, pulls the rind out,

rinses it under the faucet, hands it back. She slurps. He laughs.
      She laughs. *Carrot*, she says, mouth full. *Mango*, he teaches.
Chicken. Carrots. She yums

like she's tasting them. *Latkes.* She sucks
      the rind, grey eyes closed, kissing-closed. *Butter.*
She cat-tongues her wrist, skeleton fingers. *Noodles.* He saws

into the stringy pit. Fruit flecks. She snatches at them – he hates
      to think this – like a monkey in the zoo. *Noodles.*
Chicken. Mango. Mango! Good, Ma! Mango!

She bends her head to the counter's edge, slurps the stream of juice.
      Soup. Ma, it's mango! He'll go to the store, get more,
get a new knife. Tell the doctors. *Luckshen.*

Mango, Ma. He puts a yellow nub, almost nothing,
      in her cupped hands. She licks, hunts for more. *Shabbos?*
she says. *Mango*, he says. *Orange-orange.*

All the meat is gone now. He takes a wedge of rind
      from the garbage, a thread of orange still clinging,
runs it under water, squeezes to make juice,

keep her happy.

Jim Daniels
THOUGHTS ON THE OSCARS: KILLING IT

Wind gusts toward my mother dying 309 miles away in Detroit. Hope
it dies down before I make the final flat drive across Ohio where
nothing can stop it. If my mother was out in this, she'd be a ragged
hysterical kite. Just last week she knocked out a tooth jerking away
from the nurse forcing her to swallow pills. The Oscars tonight. Red
Carpet's already started. My mother used to love Joan Rivers. Any
female comic. All two of them — Joan and Phyllis Diller. They both
had work done. Blind now, my mother never walked or flew on a
red carpet. She promised God she wouldn't kill herself. Didn't Jesus
commit suicide? I found three rosaries under her bed. She stopped
falling because she never gets up. Why, she wants to know, should I?
The audience is stumped. Her current role is a tour de force. No one
even recognizes the sweet, generous woman she once was — nurse,
mother, caregiver. What a transformation! Five stars! That's the most,
isn't it? Or, four? She's done her last crossword puzzle over the phone.
She's listened to her last book on tape. Last year I made it to Best
Supporting Actor, then fell asleep. The wind — can she hear it? She was
a big *Tonight Show* fan when Joan hosted. My mother was always up,
beer and cigarettes, in her bright, wild muumuu on the couch. Zany
Housewife. Cackling.

No one could swirl a cigarette in the air like my mother. It killed her to
quit. It's killing her now. Magisterial with that cigarette, ash reckless
in her wake. She's a bare, skinny tree now, rootless. My parents never
went to movies — five kids at home. Fantasy, a dark, quiet room —
no need for the big screen. And yet she followed tabloids for their
steamrolling scandals, ugly photos of beautiful people. My mother had
the squawking laugh of Joan and Phyllis. She never had work done,
due to lack of funding. She did have her eyebrows tattooed on since
she couldn't draw them blind. Last time I was home, she leaned into
me on the couch until I draped my arm around her. Kill me, she said.
They're playing the music, and she's ready and willing to walk off
without accepting a thing — no statuette or stranger's arm — she's taken
the hint, but nobody's letting her offstage. The wind squall, incredible
today. If she could only cup her hands against it and light up one more
time.

Keith Taylor
IRISES IN CALIFORNIA

When I wanted to smoke,
I would step outside
the house in southern California
where my mother lay dying.

In the back yard there, in early April,
purple irises strained to open.

When their petals finally
pulled apart, I could
clearly hear the puff
of their faint exhalations.

Ellen Lord
CEMETERY WALK
—after Robert Creeley

Grief comes softly
snugs me heavy
like an old coat.

What did I know
thinking myself
alone today
without a friend—

so many voices
ride this wind.

Phillip Sterling
MERMAN

He swam to within six yards of the dock, where Audry had been tanning for nearly half an hour. She'd spent fifteen minutes on her back and now, so far, seven on her stomach, with the right side of her unblushed face pressed to the floral kitchen towel she had appropriated from the dirty laundry to use as a sweat-rag. For seven minutes she had observed nothing more than the former resort's vacant boat launch, its reedy shore and green gobs of goose shit. But when she flipped her loose-bound ponytail in the opposite direction and was about to lay her head back down —*exposing the other cheek*, she thought playfully— she noticed what appeared to be a muskrat or beaver plying the calm surface of the small lake.

She'd left her contacts in her purse; she'd left her purse in the car. Her glasses were somewhere in the book bag near her feet, as were two bottles of water, an assortment of lip gloss (both tubes and sticks), several cranberry-laced energy bars, a travel-pack of baby wipes (hypoallergenic), and the keys to her car. The bag acted as an anchor for the latest issue of *Elle*, which she'd purchased at Meijer when she stopped for gas that morning, its weight meant to prevent the magazine from blowing into the lake—despite the unlikelihood of that happening, given the absence of any wind to speak of. The only imperfections on the water's glassy surface were the small splashes and ripples generated by the creature's sluggish progress, which was somewhat painful to watch, as if the thing were exhausted or half-dead, its feet kicking—if at all—limply. Closer, Audry was surprised to see it was not an amphibious creature of any kind but rather a man, his dark, unfashionably long hair trailing like a tail of a wood duck.

It was also the moment she'd realized that her bathing suit top was only within reach if she pushed up onto her elbows and combat-crawled over to the t-shirt and hoodie she'd dropped in a careless pile when she'd reached the dock and found to her good fortune that she would be alone, that apparently no one else who knew about the public access had had the inclination to call in sick, mid-week—on what the Weather Channel predicted would be September's last 'unseasonably warm' day—to catch some late summer rays.

Not like she was obsessed about tanning, or even cared about strap lines. Not like she scheduled regular appointments for the tanning beds at the gym, like so many of the other women in her Pilates class. It wasn't about the look or color of her skin. Rather, sunbathing was something that Audry found she needed, occasionally, to help maintain a certain—for lack of a better word—*balance*. She'd discovered it in her early teens—how occasional sunning provided her with a certain respite and consolation, how it re-energized her, so to speak—the way she imagined a cat might find solace in the warmth of the compact refrigerator beside her bed, its motor calming and necessary (if only her landlord allowed pets!). Over the years sunbathing had helped Audry contend with many of the clumsy teenage and young adult traumas girls struggle with, like break-ups or hideous parental intrusions, in ways that her friends' methods— pigging-out on pizza or Häagen Dazs or scarfing a theater-sized box of Milk Duds—never did. A little sun, a little vitamin D, often made the world more manageable, made Audry feel generous and sociable.

Or so she had thought.

Now she was thinking, *Awkward*.

Nor did she appear to be alone in such thinking, as the man's progress slowed and then stopped twenty feet or so from the dock where she lay, as if he'd just realized she was there; or, as if up until then something else had occupied his mind, something like heartache or grief or loss—something that had set him off on a road trip to a place he'd never been before, down a two-track road, say, in a remote part of a state forest, and then into the water of what appeared to be a soulless lake, as if to release himself from the sorrow of his aching heart.

Or perhaps Audry was simply projecting onto him her own surprise at his appearance, what now looked like the face of a twenty-seven-year-old IT geek, the kind who—as a way to counter the dreadful mind-numbing redundancy of writing code—sought sensory stimulation in pseudo-extreme sports activities (like training for triathlons one never intends to enter). A man who clearly did not want to be caught in his deception, for he looked somewhat nonplussed, she thought, the way he treaded water awkwardly a safe distance from the dock. He looked embarrassed—as if he were in fact a merman whose legs were fused into a fin- or tail-like appendage that would prevent him from maneuvering suavely into her sphere of intimacy. In addition, he was blinking wildly, erratically, the way a person would if he were trying to clear his vision, or if he needed eyewear for distance yet had left his dark-framed glasses on top of the clothes he'd carefully folded and stacked on the far shore of the lake. Audry's face flushed with empathy. The man bobbed and resurfaced, his splashing glittered in the sun. Whether he wore light-colored bathing trunks or white Fruit-of-the-Looms or Audry had caught a glimpse of his untanned buttocks—she couldn't be sure.

Otherwise, he looked harmless enough. Even a little peakish.

Until he spoke. Or seemed to. The words were garbled.

"I'm sorry?" Audry said, her voice pitching a question.

"You *want* me," said the man in the water.

So maybe she'd misjudged the circumstances—seriously misjudged them. *Stay calm*, she told herself. Her keys—and her glasses—were in the book bag, of course, which she could easily snatch up on a run to the car—she'd left it unlocked—a car she would surely reach before he could even swim to shore. Besides, there were two one-liter bottles of spring water to throw, if need be—that might slow him down—and she'd mindfully had the foresight to toss a change of clothes on the backseat. Audry had no qualms about leaving behind her yoga pad and floral hand towel, or even the bikini top, having never really cared for its beige color anyway, its puffy little embroidered flowers...and she could always buy another *Elle*...

"Ex-*cuse* me?" Audry spat the words, to keep her voice from wavering.

"I said *I'm hungry*," the man repeated. "Would you possibly have any food? It's a longer swim than I'd thought."

"Hungry?" she echoed.

"A granola bar? Some pretzels?"

Perhaps she'd simply misheard what he'd said. Or perhaps she'd heard what she'd have liked to hear and not the actual words. Or perhaps he was playing with her, mocking her. Perhaps it was all a ploy. After all, there was the issue of her having to expose more of her body than she felt comfortable with, in reaching for her bag, where bottles of spring water would have to be rearranged in order to retrieve a single energy bar, should she wish to share one.

Had *he* realized how compromised her position was when he'd gotten close? Had he planned on it?

"Uh,…no," she lied. "Not really."

"Oh," said the man, his long hair plastered over one eye like a pirate's patch. "Okay, then." He turned as if to swim back the way he came when Audry noticed a small tattoo on his shoulder—a fish of some kind, perhaps? Pisces?

"Sorry," she said, softly, in the tone of voice she used for the Homeless-and-Anything-Will-Help woman she encountered at the corner of Michigan and Fuller nearly every day on her way to work (mouthed from inside her car, of course, when she was not able to catch a green light).

He spun in the water and faced her, his wood-duck-colored hair swept to one side, away from his eyes, yet Audry couldn't tell, from that distance, if they were green or gray. His nose and lips, however, were extraordinarily thin, fish-like.

"No, that's okay," he said. "Sorry to have bothered. I just thought…"

Well, you thought wrong, Audry mused to herself, bitterly— her bitterness directed as much at herself as at the man. But why? Because he'd appeared out of nowhere like some kind of mythological god, some Triton, interrupting her solitude and demanding her food? That she'd felt violated by the very intrusion, threatened by the circumstances? Or was it rather that he was not what she'd expected from a merman, did not show the moxie she assumed a Triton should, that he perhaps fell short as a god?

Or, worse yet, was it because he'd dismissed her so easily, had somehow found her to be lacking—a mere mortal—and not worth his effort?

Or had she simply fallen asleep and dreamt it.

She could feel her temples throb, though not in the way they had when she'd first realized a man swam toward her. Now she felt more anger than fear. The man was hardly dangerous, foundering as he was, still some distance away. And not unattractive. What difference would it make if she offered him what she had? There were three—no, *four*—energy bars in the bottom of her bag. And more than one bottle of water…not that he had asked for water—nor even had any need of water, submerged as he was. (an irony she found both funny…and disarming.) What possible harm could come from her being sociable, something she'd been told more than once she was incapable of, especially given the circumstances? She clearly had the upper hand.

Audry raised slightly on her elbows and took a small breath, ready to concede. Yet before she was able to bring words to her lips, she could see that the man had already begun swimming back the way he came, toward the far shore.

"Sorry!" she repeated, louder, addressing the duck tail of dark hair. It would be meager consolation. *Too little too late*, she told herself, *once again*.

The merman spun around a second time and faced her. "It's just…" he said. His head bobbed as his hands feathered the water, his dark hair swayed to the thrusts of his legs—if he had legs; the blue fish on his shoulder dove and rose. "I mean, don't you ever just get tired of it? Of being alone? Doesn't it sometimes make you *hungry*?"

He didn't wait for an answer. He turned a final time and swam—somewhat awkwardly—out of her sight.

Eric Torgersen
ONLY THEN

He's content, for the most part, with their life,
he knows in any case that he'll never betray her,

so he daydreams her some gentle, painless death,
himself month on month of sheer faithful desolation

(passing quickly somehow in the daydream),
and only then does he daydream himself a girl

who understands and is willing, even eager
to wait until the deep well of his conscience

has cleared at last all the way to its dark bottom,
and only then does he plead, and only with his eyes,

for the mercy of her breasts, and she grants him
every last mercy of that young body, and he

is blessed and healed in the daydream and only then
does he fall at last into deep, untroubled sleep.

Jack Ridl
IN THE PHOTOGRAPH ACROSS THE ROOM

In a browning lithograph that sits on a
wobbly end table my great grandfather
holds the reins of two slow-hoofed horses

draped in bells. He drives a beer wagon,
barrels of pilsner and lager brewed nine miles
from this very corner on a Pittsburgh twisting

hillside. But for me there is no lithograph. He's
still driving the wagon, softly calling to Jess and
Josh who know only work and a bed of straw,

two roans who once gave rides in a carnival
that carried each town's loneliness back and forth
over the Ohio for ten years, letting anyone ride:

child, grandmother, tall, fat, short, first timer,
a lying cowboy who had ridden nothing more
than an old St. Louis bar stool. Now across

the long lost trail of my memory's belief he
sits, the devotion of his dog beside him, looking
one way as he looks long down the other.

Joshua Kulseth
INHERITANCE
for Norburn Hyatt

Long step up the driver's seat
my grandfather makes
with less ease each new time —
teaching me to drive
he moves away
from one more responsibility.
We begin together:
check rotors, depress the clutch,
fire the ignition, start the blade's rotation;
slow clinking at first becoming
now a low hum
to the compliant engine.
He climbs down and waits
standing small below himself.
Unsure in my seat,
I'm waved on by his hand
and mouthed command
to ease back on the gas,
follow my own tracks.
The smell of dew and cut grass
with each new pass
assures me looking at the pasture gate,
watching him
climb the house stairs —
the rotary churns,
cut hay slumps in heaps,
bowing in my wake.

Lauren Mallett
THE OVERBLESSING

Ours is a smoky burn pile — shoulder high and more soaked through with rain than
we realized. That's your son coaxing the flames,

alternating splashes of gasoline with
ripped cardboard and crackly Scotch broom.

This is the house you built, its cedar roof, Victorian gables, pastel pinks and blues.

I'm in what was your sewing room, watching Strand from
the bay window seat. You died long before I met him and when

I circle back to the
domains of *deserve* or *luck*, he reminds me those are questions not worth considering.

You are the bathroom tiles' perfectly random florals, the fireplace rocks'
belly buttons. You are your books.

You are your hair, curled into a sandwich bag
at the bottom of the sick clothes bin in the attic.

On the top shelf of the closet we share is the box of your ashes, next to
the framed photo of you posed in front of a plate display window.

You are tan and blonde
and petite. Your domed, silver necklace and wristwatch send out their flares.

Go on, I want you to say.

I want to wear your socks.

They're not mine, I know, and so isn't so much else.
I sit and wait for the trees' green spokes to tremble, for every termite bored into
the roof to fall away

and for the world to flood back into the thousands
of holes they left,

where I over and over want to tuck in my thanks.

One big boof and then nothing, Strand calls from the foyer.
I meet him in the hallway. *Couldn't get the fire to go.*

I reach for him. I breathe into your
son's neck, when the outside of his sweat rushes into me and what you made once again I
behold.

in memory of T. Katharine Sheldahl-Thomason (1946-2003)

Michelle DeRose
ODE TO OUR WENONAH

We honeymooned in our canoe,
our L.L. Bean registry exhausted,
gear so newly purchased its gleam
garnered side-eyes and snickers
from Canadian one-trippers.
But it also clued in the park
volunteer, who ran to the dock
with permits changed to an island
with one site. We barely scratched
the craft but paddled past grouse,
between a moose and her calves,
beneath an air-borne bat
ballet, and chose to spend time
in the canoe again. And again.

An overnight anniversary paddle
on the Two Hearted led me to question
our livery driver en route to the put-in
about crowds on Hemingway's 100th
Birthday. *Who?*

Fresh from burying the Aussie
who welcomed our baby home,
we canoed the Au Sable too soon
in the spring, tipped at a cedar jam,
and assessed fleece layers among
us, both calculating how many times
our sleeves would encircle our toddler.

When it wasn't half-full of hose water
in the yard, a make-shift kiddie pool,
we loaded buckets with pebbles,
zipped packets of fruit snacks,
peanut-butter-and-honey on white,
Cheez-its, beef jerky into the dry bag.

(no break)
Stopped for rocks, swimming holes,
taut lines, geo-caches. Leashed
new puppies to the gunwale,
added PBR to the cooler.

I have learned when to draw
away from riffles, when to trust
the Wenonah to float us over
their danger. Myron has learned
I'm not always aware of the difference–
when I see in the sun's sparkle
the final throes of our last fire before
we were parents; when an anciently
gray heron angles away from the stream,
legs pointing to the past while it beaks
toward a future we can't see;
when a downed cedar morphs to my
grandmother's hand beckoning to the bank
or her grave, compelling my gaze
to its thickening branches retreating
into the wet meadow sedge.

Zoe Boyer
REWILDING

This August I returned to my hometown of Evanston, Illinois after
six years in the mountainous high desert of northern Arizona. I had
moved when the narrow strip of Lake Michigan shore abutting the
city no longer felt wild enough for the sort of nature I craved. In
Prescott, Arizona, I reveled in ponderosa forest, ephemeral creeks,
quartz crags, and arid scrub, still occasionally traveling back to the
Midwest for summer sailing. When the pandemic arrived, however,
I chose to remain rooted in the Southwest, where I could continue to
explore the vast, arterial network of trails in Prescott National Forest.

    I wasn't the only one who sought refuge in nature. While the
pandemic made the world a terrifying place, it also made it a quieter
one. Streets emptied of cars, the roar of traffic on Route 89 replaced
by birdsong and wind sifting through the leaves. An increasing
demand for fresh air and solitude led even those in the region who
weren't yet adventure-minded to the outdoors; an influx of humans
joined the mule deer, javelinas, pumas, and countless soaring,
crawling, bounding creatures who call the forest home.

    Returning to Evanston after spending so long with only
the wilderness for company has spawned a mountain of mixed
emotions—the only elevation in a prairie-flat land. I find myself
overwhelmed by the noise, the swarms of people, the smells. Cars
rattle the floors at all hours, clattering over speed bumps and blaring
their basses at ear-quaking volume. The lakefront is a crush of bodies,
and the resinous scent of ponderosas has been replaced with exhaust,
cigarette smoke, and the ersatz flowers of perfumes. But as I adjust to
the sensory onslaught, I've begun to notice something new.

    Evanston has gone through a sort of urban rewilding over
the course of the pandemic. Where suburban lawns once carved
the town into neat, green facets, pollinator gardens now flourish,
rife with native grasses and wildflowers: the orange origami buds of
butterfly weed, cheerful black-eyed Susans, and riots of echinacea in
every shade of sunrise. Yard signs read, "Please excuse our weeds,
we're feeding the bees," and sure enough, the bees are feasting.
My neighbor has erected columns of pastel hives on the roof of his
porch and can often be spotted wandering the neighborhood with a
bin in hand and an eye towards the trees, looking to catch an errant

swarm. Monarchs, their numbers straggling in previous years, have returned to the land in fluttering clouds of stained-glass wings, and more goldfinches than I've ever seen rustle citrus-bright amid the coneflowers.

Originally a drainage canal for the North Branch of the Chicago River, the North Shore Channel—once disparagingly and accurately referred to simply as "the sewage canal"—now flows a lucent aquamarine. Along a section of the channel's shoreline known as Harbert-Payne Woods, local volunteers have been working to remove invasive buckthorn in order to allow cottonwood, walnut, cherry, and redbud trees to flourish, providing better forage for local fauna, and making way for more native plantings. In this narrow strip of forest, branches form a shadow-laced tunnel, and stalks of pokeweed sprout bold and violently pink, their berries—poisonous to humans, but an important source of food for mockingbirds, northern cardinals, and mourning doves—on the cusp of ripening to a deep indigo.

Along a sprawling stretch of shore that was once barren sand, the Clark Street Beach Bird Sanctuary has matured to a dense spread of flora including switchgrass, rough blazing star, and common milkweed blossoming in great pom-poms of ballet-slipper pink. The sanctuary was established in 2015, just a few years before I left, when a last vestige of natural forest to the west of the Northwestern University Sailing Center was hewn to make way for a behemoth parking structure.

I had worked at the sailing center and seen how the forest's cottonwoods, box elders, hackberry trees, and shrubby sand willows served as a way station for migrating birds, and for the dragonflies who arrived in great clouds of blue each summer to put on a dazzling show as I lay on the trampoline of a catamaran beneath the shimmer of their cellophane wings. The trees were also home to warrens of rabbits, and a sprightly fox who often left "gifts" for us to find on the sand—the grisly remains of his nocturnal meals that we rushed to dispose of before campers arrived. I had been devastated to lose this last, wooded refuge in an increasingly urbanized town, so to see trees returned to the shore by dedicated volunteers—their branches now filled with cedar waxwings, goldfinches, and palm warblers—rekindles a hope so often dampened by the insidious creep of concrete.

68

I still miss the rural high desert—the hush of hot air stirred by grasshopper wings, mule deer grazing beside a creek swollen with monsoon rain. But I'm learning to embrace this urban wildness, to appreciate the sweat-slicked toil of a community working to restore balance to an ecosystem so far removed from the natural order. I know American bird populations are still in rapid decline, their migratory paths increasingly stripped and squared to a patchwork quilt of pavement, lawn, and agricultural land that feeds so few. But as I write this, I'm watching the neighbor's garden through my window, and where there was once nothing more than a threadbare swath of mown grass, goldfinches, cardinals, chickadees, and sparrows are flittering through waves of goldenrod.

Shutta Crum
THE CLOTH OF THIS LIFE

Once, if you'd placed your hand inside my life
you would have felt burlap, or homespun cotton —
a roughness necessary for the stuff of sturdy living.

These days, you'll feel the worn patience
of an old dishtowel. Of days spent tidying up,
or wiping the world dry when weeping spilled over.

Washed and hung to lift in summer winds,
this life's grown thin and soft — faded to an indecipherable blue.
The years have rubbed off nubs from my rough fiber.
Feel that? It's a life so fine clouds float through it.

Carrie Strand Tebeau
KITCH-ITI-KIPI

Mirror, mirror in the ground
what's shaped like something deep and round?

If you hear an echo, you must repeat it.

If you see a reflection, you must reflect on it.

If a small lake takes the sky and wears it like a skin then you must
choose a cloud and jump in.

CONTRIBUTOR BIOS

TERRY BOHNHORST BLACKHAWK'S poetry collections include *Escape Artist*, winner of the 2002 John Ciardi Prize; *One Less River*, a Kirkus Reviews Best 2019 title; and *Maumee, Maumee* (Alice Greene, 2022). Recipient of the Pablo Neruda Prize and a Kresge fellowship, she has recent work in *Brevity*, *Verse Daily*, *Vox Populi*, and *Paterson Literary Review*.

ZOE BOYER was raised in Evanston, Illinois on the shore of Lake Michigan, and completed her MA in creative writing among the ponderosa pines in Prescott, Arizona. Her work has appeared in such publications as *The New York Times*, *Poetry South*, *Kelp Journal*, *Plainsongs*, *About Place*, and *West Trade Review*.

ABIGAIL CLOUD is a teaching professor at Bowling Green State University, from which she holds an MFA in poetry. She is the editor-in-chief of *Mid-American Review*. Her collection, *Sylph*, won the Lena-Miles Wever Todd Prize and was published by Pleiades Press in 2014.

* SHUTTA CRUM has won eight Royal Palm Literary Awards. She's had 150+ poems published, been nominated for a Pushcart Prize, and authored eighteen traditionally published books for children and three chapbooks of poetry. *When You Get Here* won a gold Royal Palm. *Meet Me Out There* is her latest chapbook.

* JIM DANIELS' latest book, *The Luck of the Fall*, fiction, was published in 2023. Recent poetry books include *The Human Engine at Dawn* and *Gun/Shy*. His chapbook, *Comment Card*, will be published in 2024. A native of Detroit, he lives in Pittsburgh and teaches in the Alma College MFA program.

* DANI KNOPH DAVIS attended the School of Art & Design at the University of Michigan and later relocated to Seattle. In 2012, she returned to Northern Michigan where she continues to develop a collection of Michigan wildlife illustrations.

* MICHELLE DEROSE, Professor of English at Aquinas College, is the 2023 winner of the Faruq Z Bey award. Find her poetry in the anthologies *Where We Left Our Last Few Words: 50 Years in Tully Cross*, *G. I. Days: An Anthology of Military Life*, and in several journals.

* JOHN FLESHER is a retired Associated Press reporter based in Traverse City, Michigan, whose journalism focuses primarily on the environment, politics and government. He was a Ted Scripps fellow in environmental journalism at the University of Colorado. His literary essays have appeared in *Dunes Review* and *Traverse* magazine.

* LINDA NEMEC FOSTER is the author of over twelve collections of poetry including recent books *Bone Country* and *The Blue Divide*. The inaugural Poet Laureate of Grand Rapids, she won first prize in the 2023 Allen Ginsberg Poetry Award. Her new work appears in *Vox Populi* and *Best Small Fictions*.

BRYN GRIBBEN is a poet and essayist who left academia to explore antiques. She was a finalist for the Creative Nonfiction Porch Prize and for the Peseroff Prize in poetry. Read her musical memoir, *Amplified Heart: An Emotional Discography*. Bryn lives in Seattle with two cats and one husband.

* DAVID HARDIN is the author of the memoir *Standpipe, Delivering Water in Flint* (Belt Publishing), a 2022 Michigan Notable Book.

* ELIZABETH KERLIKOWSKE volunteers at Gateway Academy in Gull Lake. She wrote this poem to make both grammar and poetry more fun for alternative high school students. Her latest chapbook is "The Woodworker and the Witch."

* JOSHUA KULSETH earned his BA in English from Clemson University, his MFA in poetry from Hunter College, and his PhD in poetry from Texas Tech University. His poems have appeared in several journals. His poetry manuscript, *Leaving Troy*, is forthcoming from Finishing Line Press. He teaches at Clemson University.

NATHAN LIPPS is the author of *the body as passage* and *Built Around the Fire* (forthcoming, 2024). His work has appeared in *Best New Poets, Colorado Review, EcoTheo Review, North American Review, TYPO*, and *Third Coast*. Read more at his website.

JOEL LONG's book *Winged Insects* won the White Pine Press Poetry Prize. *Lessons in Disappearance* and *Knowing Time by Light* were published by Blaine Creek Press. Elk Press published chapbooks *Chopin's Preludes* and *Saffron Beneath Every Frost*. His poems and essays appear in several journals. He lives in Salt Lake City.

* ELLEN LORD is a Northern Michigan native whose writing appears in *Dunes Review, Walloon Writers Review, U.P. Reader,* and *Haiku Society of America*. She is a behavioral health therapist, specializing in addiction and trauma. She resides in Charlevoix County and Trout Creek, Michigan. Find her chapbook, *Relative Sanity* (2023) at **ellenlordauthor.com**.

LAUREN MALLETT's poems appear in *Poetry Northwest, Puerto del Sol, The Seventh Wave, The Night Heron Barks* and other journals. She lives on Clatsop land of Oregon's north coast. **www.laurenmallett.com**

* MICHAEL MARK is the author of Rattle Chapbook Prize winner *Visiting Her in Queens is More Enlightening than a Month in a Monastery in Tibet*. Recent poems appear in *Best American Poetry Blog, Copper Nickel, Ploughshares, Pleiades, Poetry Northwest, Salt Hill, Sixth Finch, The Southern Review, The Sun,* and *32 Poems*. **Michaeljmark.com**

ABHISHEK MEHTA is a marketing professional with a discreet passion for putting words together in a way that they may be able to hold his short and sudden glances in their direction. His writing has previously appeared in *South Florida Poetry Journal, Inkwell Journal* and *Meow Meow Pow Pow Lit.*

ERIC P. MUELLER lives in Alameda, CA. His essays and reviews have appeared in *Talking River, Gold Man Review, Pyre Magazine, Foglifter, Pyre Magazine, Longleaf Review, The Ignatian, Vagabond City Review*, and elsewhere. Reading outside, pop punk music, red blends, and soft pretzels are some of his favorite things.

BARBRA NIGHTINGALE's 10th book of poetry, *Spells & Other Ways of Flying* (Kelsay Books, 2021), was a Distinguished Favorite in the 2022 Independent Press Awards. Her poems have appeared in journals such as *Rattle, Narrative Magazine, Witchery, Florida Review.* She is an Associate Editor with the *South Florida Poetry Journal.*

DAVID A. PORTER is a graduate of Rutgers University and San Francisco State University, where he received his MFA in Creative Writing. Porter was a co-founder and the managing editor of 20 Pounds of *Headlights*, a literary annual published in San Francisco in 2004. He lives in New York.

* GREG RAPPLEYE's collection, *A Path Between Houses* (University of Wisconsin Press, 2000), won the Brittingham Prize. *Figured Dark* (University of Arkansas Press, 2007), won the Arkansas Prize, and *Tropical Landscape with Ten Hummingbirds* (Dos Madres Press, 2018), won the Arts & Letters Prize in *Poetry*. He lives in Grand Haven, Michigan.

JC REILLY is the author of the full-length collection, *What Magick May Not Alter*, and three other books. She is Co-Editor of *Atlanta Review*. Follow her on Twitter @aishatonu, on Bluesky @aishatonu.bsky.social, or on Insta @jc.reilly.

* Two of JACK RIDL's books have been named Collection of the Year, one by the Association of Midland Authors, one by *ForeWord Review*s. His collection *All at Once* is forthcoming from CavanKerry Press. The Carnegie Foundation named him Michigan's Professor of the Year. More than 100 of his students are published.

AMANDA RUSSELL is an editor at *The Comstock Review* and a stay-at-home mom. Her poems appear in *Hole in the Head re:View, EcoTheo Review, Lily Poetry Review*, and *Open: a Journal of Arts and Letters*. To learn about her or her chapbook, *Barren Years*, visit **https://poetrussell.wordpress.com/**.

* NANCY SQUIRES is a writer, lawyer, and freelance copy editor. Her creative nonfiction and poetry have appeared in *Dunes Review, Blueline Magazine, Split Rock Review*, and *Writers Resist*. She lives in Michigan.

* GARRETT STACK's first book is *Yeoman's Work* (Bottom Dog Press, 2020). His poems were most recently published in *The Pinch, Blue Earth Review,* and *Sand Lake Literary Magazine.* He works, writes, and will die Middle Western.

JOANNIE STANGELAND is the author of several collections, including *The Scene You See* (Ravenna Press). Her poems have also appeared in *Atlanta Review, Meridian, The Pedestal Magazine, The Worcester Review, The MacGuffin,* and other journals. Joannie holds an MFA from the Rainier Writing Workshop.

* PHILLIP STERLING's most recent book is *Local Congregation: Poems Uncollected 1985-2015.* His collection of essays and memoir, *Lessons in Geography: The Education of a Michigan Poet* is scheduled for publication later this year.

* ELLEN STONE advises Poetry Club at Community High School in Ann Arbor, Michigan, co-hosts a monthly poetry series, *Skazat!* and co-edits *Public School Poetry,* a literary journal. She is the author of *The Solid Living World* (Michigan Writers' Cooperative Press, 2013) and *What Is in the Blood* (Mayapple Press, 2020).

* CARRIE STRAND TEBEAU is a poet and fiber artist living in Northern Michigan, where she is Associate Director of the Good Hart Artist Residency. She's a previous winner of *Dunes Review*'s William J. Shaw Memorial prize.

FM STRINGER has an MFA in Poetry from the University of Maryland. His writing can be found in *BRUISER, B O D Y, jmww,* and elsewhere. He lives in Pennsylvania with his wife and two dogs.

*ALISON SWAN's collection, *A Fine Canopy,* was shortlisted for an IPPY, named one of LitHub's most anticipated 2020 books, and recommended by Orion magazine. *Fresh Water: Women Writing on the Great Lakes,* is a Michigan Notable Book. She has received a Mesa Refuge Residency and the Petoskey Prize for Environmental Leadership.

* KEITH TAYLOR has two books in 2024: *All the Time I Want: Selected Poems 1977 - 2017* appeared in January from Dzanc Books; and a collection of new poems, *What Can the Matter Be?,* will be out in the Fall in the Made in Michigan series from Wayne State University Press.

* ERIC TORGERSEN taught writing for 38 years at Central Michigan. He and his wife Ann Kowaleski have been coming to their cottage on Green Lake, Interlochen, since 1987. In retirement he continues to write and to translate German poetry, especially that of Rainer Maria Rilke and Nicolas Born.

* ELLEN WELCKER is the author of *Ram Hands* (Scablands Books, 2016), *The Botanical Garden* (Astrophil Press, 2010) and five chapbooks, including *Keep Talking* (Sixth Finch Books, 2023). She lives in the US midwest and is online at **ellenwelcker.com.**

RAE ZALOPANY is a Tampa Bay native writer. She recently graduated and received her MFA from the University of South Florida for fiction and comics. Her work can be found at *Michigan Quarterly Review, The Boiler, Cut Bank, South East Review,* and elsewhere.

READER BIOS

*KELLI FITZPATRICK is an author and editor from Michigan currently earning an MFA in Creative Writing and Environment at Iowa State University. Her fiction has been published by Simon and Schuster, *Flash Fiction Online,* and others. Her editing credits include work for Modiphius Entertainment and San Jose State University. Website: **KelliFitzpatrick.com**

*CHRIS GIROUX received his doctorate from Wayne State University and is a professor of English at Saginaw Valley State University, where he has served as faculty advisor for the school's literary magazine and co-founded the community arts journal *Still Life.* His second chapbook, *Sheltered in Place,* was released in 2022.

*ANNE-MARIE OOMEN's memoir, *As Long As I Know You: The Mom Book* won the AWP Sue Silverman Nonfiction Award. She has also written *Lake Michigan Mermaid* with Linda Nemec Foster (Michigan Notable Book), *Love, Sex and 4-H* (Next Generation Indie Award for Memoir), and others.

*JOHN MAUK has published a range of stories and nonfiction works. He has a PhD in rhetoric from Bowling Green State University. His first full collection, *Field Notes for the Earthbound,* is available on Black Lawrence Press. He currently hosts Prose from the Underground, a YouTube video series for working writers. For more information, see johnmauk.com.

*TERESA SCOLLON's recent publications include the poetry collection *Trees and Other Creatures* (Alice Greene) and an essay in *Elemental,* an anthology of Michigan essayists (Wayne State University Press). A National Endowment for the Arts fellow, she teaches the Writers Studio program at North Ed Career Tech in Traverse City.

*JENNIFER YEATTS' literary life has included MA and MFA degrees in poetry, teaching writing in various forms, and editorial roles at *Passages North* and *Fugue.* She is the director of the Higher Grounds Coffee Learning Lab.

SUBMISSION GUIDELINES

Dunes Review welcomes work from writers at all stages of their careers living anywhere in the world, though we particularly love featuring those with ties to Michigan and the Midwest. We are open to all styles and aesthetics, but please read the following carefully to dive a little deeper into what we're looking for.

Ultimately, we're looking for work that draws us in from the very first line: with image, with sound, with sense, with lack of sense. We're looking for writing that makes us *feel* and bowls us over, lifts us up, and takes us places we've never been to show us ordinary things in ways we've never seen them. We're looking for poems and stories and essays that teach us how to read them and pull us back to their beginnings as soon as we've read their final lines. We're looking for things we can't wait to read again, things we can't wait to share with the nearest person who will listen. Send us your best work. We'll give it our best attention.

Submissions are accepted only via our Submittable platform: www.dunesreview.submittable.com. We do not consider work sent through postal mail or email. Any submissions sent through email will not be read or responded to. Please see further guidelines posted on our site. We look forward to reading your work!

Join our community of Michigan Writers!

Annual membership: $40 / Student rate: $20

Membership includes:

• Our monthly email newsletter to stay up to date with events;

• Two annual issues of *Dunes Review*, Northern Michigan's premier literary journal;

• Free admission to Michigan Writers workshops;

• Eligibility for the annual Michigan Writers Cooperative Press chapbook contest for first-time authors;

• Eligibility for scholarships to select conferences and retreats, such as the summer Interlochen Writers' Retreat;

• And ... well, since we're an organization of members, you decide!

To become a member, visit www.michwriters.org/join

Call for Patrons

Dunes Review is a not-for-profit endeavor to promote creative work within the Northern Michigan writing community and beyond.

The cost of publication can be underwritten in part by individual contributions. We invite you to support the publication of the next issue with a donation of $50.

Send your check payable to **Michigan Writers** to:
Michigan Writers, P.O. Box 2355 Traverse City, MI 49685

Thank you in advance for your support! Questions? Contact us at info@michwriters.org.

Printed in the USA
CPSIA information can be obtained
at www.ICGtesting.com
JSHW021209200224
57559JS00003B/20